SOAR!

SOAR!
Follow Your Dreams

June Cotner

Andrews McMeel
Publishing®

Kansas City • Sydney • London

SOAR!

Andrews McMeel Publishing, LLC
an Andrews McMeel Universal company
1130 Walnut Street, Kansas City, Missouri 64106

www.andrewsmcmeel.com

15 16 17 18 19 WKT 10 9 8 7 6 5 4

ISBN: 978-1-4494-4972-8

Library of Congress Control Number: 2013950698

Book design by Holly Ogden

ATTENTION: SCHOOLS AND BUSINESSES
Andrews McMeel books are available at quantity discounts with
bulk purchase for educational, business, or sales promotional use.
For information, please e-mail the Andrews McMeel Publishing
Special Sales Department: specialsales@amuniversal.com.

If you can dream it,
You can do it.

Dedicated to dreamers everywhere.

May we all be inspired and
create highways to our dreams!

contents

four
PERSEVERANCE 51

five

EXCELLENCE 63

eight
DAILY REMINDERS 125

letter to readers

Whether we're graduating from a learning institution
or pursuing a new dream, finding the inspiration to step
confidently into the unknown is an important part of our
personal growth. Knowing that others have persevered in
following their dreams—and taking heart from their words
of wisdom—is the perfect way to discover our own ability
to soar.

When it comes to achieving your potential, *SOAR!
Follow Your Dreams* is full of motivational thoughts and words
of encouragement to help you along your way. The book
is divided by chapter into selections that can apply to your
dreams, your choices, persevering when things get tough,
and excellence. There are also shorter thoughts to serve as
daily reminders for success.

One of the useful aspects of *SOAR!* is that it focuses on
how *you* can follow your dreams. Making your own choices,
believing in yourself, and acting courageously are all
consistent messages throughout the book. When we put our
dreams into action (especially at turning points in our lives),
we as individuals can make a difference in the world.

In *SOAR! Follow Your Dreams* you will discover moving
and motivational selections from classic writers and
successful individuals such as Aristotle, Confucius, Albert

Einstein, Ralph Waldo Emerson, Anne Frank, Mahatma Gandhi, Pablo Picasso, and Eleanor Roosevelt, as well as new and original content from contributors including Corrine De Winter, Theresa Mary Grass, Emily Ruth Hazel, Paul Keenan, and Arlene Gay Levine.

I have been compiling anthologies for more than twenty years and currently have a list of more than 900 writers who contribute their poems, prayers, and prose to my books. *SOAR!* is a combination of classic words as well as new content, and I believe you will find many refreshing and inspirational selections between its covers.

The pieces in this book have been carefully selected to apply to a variety of goals and achievements in your life, such as graduating from high school or college, starting a new job, or making any major change that would benefit from the positive messages and encouragement of people who've gone before you.

thanks

I was thrilled when Patty Rice, my editor at Andrews McMeel Publishing, asked if I would be interested in creating a compilation of motivational selections on the general topic of following your dreams. I had already been working on such an idea for about eight years, so I was delighted that these words of inspiration would find their way into this book.

I am enormously grateful for Patty's presence in my life. We have been working on collections since 1997, and this will now be my seventh book with Andrews McMeel.

I'm also thankful for my two agents, Denise Marcil and Anne Marie O'Farrell, at Marcil-O'Farrell Literary. I have worked with Denise since 1990 and with Anne Marie since 2011. I love our creative brainstorming sessions, and I greatly appreciate all of the excellent ideas they bring to my work. They have truly helped me follow my dreams.

My heartfelt gratitude goes to my husband, Jim Graves, and my many relatives and friends who encourage and inspire me every day.

And lastly, I'm grateful to God who puts me in touch with so many wonderful contributors without whom my anthologies would not exist.

one

NEW DIRECTIONS

Wherever you go,
go with all your heart.

CONFUCIUS

Commencement

After all the late nights pressing words
through your pores, the door of your mind
is still propped open. There is not one final
arrival, no last step that lifts you to the top floor.
But now and then, there is a landing—
like this one—where you can pause
to catch your breath.

Though you cannot see the summit,
plant your muddy boots
and stand against the wind.
Take in the distance you've traveled—
then keep climbing.
No one tells a mountain, *Your head is in the clouds;*
come down to where the rest of us live.
Instead, we carry dreams and prayers
as water to sustain us on the journey.

Though the shoreline also has no end,
walk until the water has swallowed the light.
Let the ocean's edge remind you,
you can always reinvent yourself.

Now you begin again, your life an untwisting
of continual beginnings—the way a spider plant,
whose roots have outgrown the pot,
releases a cascade of offspring,
all those green legs reaching for the ground.

∽ EMILY RUTH HAZEL

The Call

Do you hear it?
Urging you past the portals
of yesterday, something
calls your name, dares you
to step beyond the threshold
of now into tomorrow's mystery,
the one only you can solve,
with the magic only you can make
of your one sacred life.

~ Arlene Gay Levine

Your Calling

Your calling isn't something that somebody can tell you about. It's what you feel. It's a part of your life force. It is the thing that gives you juice. The thing that you are supposed to do. And nobody can tell you what that is. You know it inside yourself.

∽ OPRAH WINFREY

New Directions

All that newfound knowledge bubbling in your head. You are ready to enter the world, begin a new job, make your mark in the world. You are intelligent and will make wise choices because you are someone who leads with your heart. You have an open mind and an open heart full of kindness and consideration. Follow your heart; the rest falls into place. Gain strength by appreciating those around you. Do not be envious of what others have because you are rich in spirit and have much to offer. Continue to learn, laugh, and discover. Work hard, love what you do, smile often.

~ SHERRI WAAS SHUNFENTHAL

Wings

Now you are perched on the edge,
looking down between the branches
at the new grass and the sparkle of the sun
on the water far below,
the river flowing swiftly, on its way
to places you have yet to see.
Trust that when you're ready to let go,
your wings will discover themselves.

∽ EMILY RUTH HAZEL

Find Yourself

Explore the earth as you now find it.
Solve new mysteries; find the stone.
Crawl to where the sphere turns firmament.
Isolate to know for certain you are not alone.
Touch the wedding of the waters,
See the elements combine.
Read the wordless book of nature
Where the spirit's clearly writ.
Make the modern magic thine.
Go, my child, into the world.
Find yourself in knowing it.

∽ MAUREEN TOLMAN FLANNERY

Explore

We have all been placed on this earth to discover
our own path, and we will never be happy if we live
someone else's idea of life.

∾ JAMES VAN PRAAGH

When young people tell me they don't know what
they want to do with their lives, I explain that they
should concentrate on finding out about life first.
Some people have to try several directions before they
find the one that is right for them. There is nothing
wrong about this.

∾ DR. JOYCE BROTHERS

The greatest thing in this world is not so much where
we stand, as in what direction we are moving.

∾ OLIVER WENDELL HOLMES, JR.

The people who get on in this world are the ones who
look for the circumstances they want, and, if they
can't find them, make them.

∾ GEORGE BERNARD SHAW

Waiting for You

As you set this new course ahead,
possibilities are boundless
and your future limitless.

No one can stop your momentum
as you take these next steps
into the future your heart is creating.

May the dreams you've kept safe in your heart
keep leading you boldly through life.

How this world has been waiting for YOU!

∽ ANNE CALODICH FONE

New Experiences Ahead

When traveling
across the
borderline from
the familiar to
the unknown,
an open mind
is the best traveling companion.
Dress for the unpredictable,
as everything is subject to change.
Remember,
when you leave the wilderness of
new experience,
take only what you
learn from it,
and leave only footprints
so others may find the way.

∾ SUSAN KOEFOD

Destination

No one knows
where they are going.
We only know
we're on a journey
to our own true selves.

∽ JOAN NOËLDECHEN

Destiny

You may be moved in a direction
You do not understand,
Away from the safe, the familiar,
Toward a vision that is blurry,
Yet still pounds against
The doors of your dreams,
Prays for recognition,
Petitions for understanding,
Whispers for acceptance.
Out toward distant possibilities,
You are propelled by a fire,
You will never fully comprehend,
But cannot extinguish.

∾ SUSAN ROGERS NORTON

Go Forth

Go forth in every direction—
for the happiness, the harmony,
the welfare of the many.
Offer your heart, the seeds of
your own understanding
like a lamp overturned
and relit again
illuminating the darkness.

∾ THE BUDDHA

two

CHOICES

What would you do if you weren't afraid?
SPENCER JOHNSON

Feathers

feathers
I often find
while walking
remind me
I can always
decide to fly

∼ VIRGINIA BARRETT

Opportunities

Creativity is God's gift to you.
What you do with it is your gift to God.

∾ BOB MOAWAD

People will try to tell you that all the great
opportunities have been snapped up. In reality,
the world changes every second, blowing new
opportunities in all directions, including yours.

∾ KEN HAKUTA

Opportunities don't knock at all. They don't have
to, they're already all around us. It's up to us to see
where they are and take advantage of them.

∾ DAVE THOMAS

Small opportunities are often the beginning of great
enterprises.

∾ DEMOSTHENES

Ars Longa, Vita Brevis

Art Is Long, Life Is Short

Like the sculptor
who chips away
at what is not
the sculpture,
your life
is in your hands,
the pure
imperfect stone
waiting for its
daily touch,
the gentle tap,

the savored strike
toward mass
and space
that form
the perfect past,
your tribute
to the art
of living.

∾ CHARLES GHIGNA

Passion

Let yourself be silently drawn by the strange pull of what you really love. It will not lead you astray.

∾ RUMI

Before you tell your life what you intend to do with it, listen for what it intends to do with you.

∾ PARKER J. PALMER

When you enjoy your life, the lines between work and play begin to blur. We do what we love and love what we do.

∾ JOHN C. MAXWELL

There are many things in life that will catch your eye, but only a few things will catch your heart. Pursue those!

∾ MICHAEL NOLAN

Our Foundation

What we are today
comes from
our thoughts of yesterday,
and our present thoughts
build our life
of tomorrow:

Our life is the creation of our mind.

∽ THE BUDDHA

Our Attitude

Our lives are not determined by what happens to us, but by how we react to what happens; not by what life brings to us, but by the attitude we bring to life. A positive attitude causes a chain reaction of positive thoughts, events, and outcomes. It is a catalyst— a spark that creates extraordinary results.

∽ AUTHOR UNKNOWN

Be Yourself

Be yourself; everyone else is already taken.

    ∾ OSCAR WILDE

To be yourself in a world that is constantly trying to make you something else is the greatest accomplishment.

    ∾ RALPH WALDO EMERSON

Follow your inner moonlight; don't hide the madness.

    ∾ ALLEN GINSBERG

You were born an original. Don't die a copy.

    ∾ JOHN MASON

Choose Wisely

Whether you are a success or failure in life has little to do with your circumstances; it has much more to do with your choices.

∾ NIDO QUBEIN

One's philosophy is not best expressed in words; it is expressed in the choices one makes. In the long run, we shape our lives and we shape ourselves.

∾ ELEANOR ROOSEVELT

Find your true path. It's so easy to become someone we don't want to be, without even realizing it's happening. We are created by the choices we make every day.

∾ DR. BERNIE S. SIEGEL

Begin with that most terrifying of all things, a clean slate. And then look, every day, at the choices you are making and when you ask yourself why you are making them, find this answer: for me, for me.

∾ ANNA QUINDLEN

Discover

Twenty years from now you will be more disappointed by the things that you didn't do than by the ones you did do. So throw off the bowlines. Sail away from the safe harbor. Catch the trade winds in your sails. Explore. Dream. Discover.

∾ AUTHOR UNKNOWN

three

DREAMS

*Every great dream
begins with a dreamer.*

HARRIET TUBMAN

Believe in Something

Believing in something
Is half of making it come true.
The other half is not letting anything
Stop you.

∽ CORRINE DE WINTER

Believe

Believe in something larger than yourself.

∾ BARBARA BUSH

It's so important to believe in yourself. Believe that you can do it, under any circumstances. Because if you believe you can, then you really will.

∾ WALLY "FAMOUS" AMOS

[People] often become what they believe themselves to be. If I believe I cannot do something, it makes me incapable of doing it. But when I believe I can, then I acquire the ability to do it even if I didn't have it in the beginning.

∾ MAHATMA GANDHI

If you believe you can, you might. If you know you can, you will.

∾ STEVE MARABOLI

Now

If there were ever a time to dare,
To make a difference,
To embark on something worth doing,
It is now.
Not for any grand cause, necessarily—
But for something that tugs at your heart,
Something that is worth your aspiration,
Something that is your dream.
You owe it to yourself
To make your days count.
Have fun. Dig deep. Stretch.

Dream big.

Know, though,
That things worth doing
Seldom come easy.
There will be times when you want to
Turn around
Pack it up and call it quits.

Those times tell you
That you are pushing yourself
And that you are not afraid to learn by trying.

Persist.

Because with an idea,
Determination and the right tools,
You can do great things.
Let your instincts, your intellect
And let your heart guide you.

Trust.

Believe in the incredible power
Of the human mind
Of doing something that makes a difference
Of working hard
Of laughing and hoping
Of lasting friends
Of all the things that will cross your path.

Next year
The start of something new
Brings the hope of something great.
Anything is possible.
There is only one you
And you will pass this way only once.
Do it right.

∽ AUTHOR UNKNOWN

Dream Big

You see things; and you say, "Why?" But I dream things that never were; and I say, "Why not?"

         ❧ GEORGE BERNARD SHAW

Reach high, for stars lie hidden in your soul.
Dream deep, for every dream precedes the goal.

         ❧ PAMELA VAULL STARR

Dream lofty dreams, and as you dream, so shall you become.

         ❧ JAMES ALLEN

Shoot for the moon. Even if you miss, you'll land among the stars.

         ❧ LES BROWN

Transformation

Cherish your imagination.
It will create an ocean of possibilities,
and lead to unexpected places.

Hold on to your dreams.
For tenacity is the force
that will anchor your visions,
to create a reality that once seemed impossible.

∾ BARB MAYER

Albert Einstein on Imagination

Imagination is more important than knowledge.
For knowledge is limited to all we now know and
understand, while imagination embraces the entire
world, and all there ever will be to know and
understand.

∾

Logic will get you from A to B.
Imagination will take you everywhere.

∾

Your imagination is your preview of life's coming
attractions.

Passages

Far more than a number of years completed,
far more than hats thrown to the wind.
It's a time of creation, change, confusion
. . . and most of all, a time of transition.

From being taken care of,
to being the caretaker.

From absorbing ideas,
to creating ideas.

From following the path of others,
to creating a path that others strive to follow.

From dreaming your life,
to living your dreams.

There are those who seek to advise you,
but in the end you must listen to your own voice.

Discover your passion,
draw from your inner strengths,
and quietly, but surely,
pursue your dreams—
with all the determination you can muster.

∽ Barb Mayer

Tag Your Dreams

Play tag
with your dreams.
Chase them
till you're breathless.
Dreams
have strong legs,
but so do you.
Keep running,
with your arm out,
fingers reaching.
Don't let them get away.

∽ JACQUELINE JULES

Sanctuary

Let your soul create
a sanctuary where
all dreams are possible
and life is grand as God's glory.
The beach stretches
before you.
You are strong as the sea's song.
Whitecaps travel and return.
May you never
feel alone or
lose sight of the
sacred seasons of your soul.

∽ PAULA TIMPSON

Dreams into Action

The world needs dreamers and the world needs doers.
But above all, the world needs dreamers who do.

     ∾ SARAH BAN BREATHNACH

We must dare to dream great dreams—
and then we must dare to put them into action.

     ∾ PETER MacDONALD

You are never given a dream without also being given
the power to make it true. You may have to work for
it, however.

     ∾ RICHARD BACH

Let your dreams be the springboard for great actions.

∽ LIESL VAZQUEZ

What we think, or what we know, or what we believe, is, in the end, of little consequence. The only thing of consequence is what we do.

∽ JOHN RUSKIN

Enthusiasm is the greatest asset in the world.
It beats money and power and influence.

∽ HENRY CHESTER

Life is not about discovering our talents; it is about pushing our talents to the limit and discovering our genius.

∽ ROBERT BRAULT

Artists

The most visible creators I know of are those artists whose medium is life itself. The ones who express the inexpressible—without brush, hammer, clay, or guitar. They neither paint nor sculpt—their medium is being. Whatever their presence touches has increased life. They see and don't have to draw. They are artists of being alive.

~ J. Stone

Your Vision

Each of us is an artist, capable of conceiving and creating a vision from the depths of our being.

~ DOROTHY FADIMAN

Visualize this thing you want. See it, feel it, believe in it. Make your mental blueprint and begin.

~ ROBERT COLLIER

Every great dream begins with a dreamer. Always remember, you have within you the strength, the patience, and the passion to reach for the stars to change the world.

~ HARRIET TUBMAN

Whatever your dreams are, start taking them very, very seriously.

~ BARBARA SHER

A Great Purpose

When you are inspired by some great purpose, some extraordinary project, all your thoughts break their bounds: your mind transcends limitations, your consciousness expands in every direction, and you find yourself in a new, great, and wonderful world. Dormant forces, faculties, and talents become alive, and you discover yourself to be a greater person by far than you ever dreamed yourself to be.

~ PATANJALI

Your Future

The best way to predict your future is to create it.

~ ABRAHAM LINCOLN

The only way to discover the limits of the possible is to go beyond them into the impossible.

~ ARTHUR C. CLARKE

The future belongs to those who believe in the beauty of their dreams.

~ ELEANOR ROOSEVELT

Even if our efforts of attention seem for years to be producing no results, one day a light that is in exact proportion to them will flood the soul.

~ SIMONE WEIL

Philosophy

Be a seeker of visions—
And a hunter of dreams.
Be alert and excited
And proud of your life.
Dance with all music
And sing with all songs.
Be awestruck with wonder
And inspired by nature.
Shun what is wrong;
Show wisdom and class.
Honor each promise;
Love friend and foe.
Laugh with the happy
And cry with the sad—
Live for tomorrow—
But save yesterday.
Run with the wind
And savor the moment.

ᑐ JOAN STEPHEN

A Blessing for Your Dreams

May your plans unfold as you dream them,
    your humility grow with success,
    your feet dance long past the music,
    and your heart expand with your purse.

∾ MARYANNE HANNAN

Your Imagination

Your imagination is yours and yours alone. You have the inborn capacity to use it in any way that you choose. No one else is responsible for your imagination. Anything placed in your imagination and held there ultimately becomes your reality.

∾ Dr. Wayne W. Dyer

Goals

A goal is a dream with a deadline.

～ NAPOLEON HILL

Obstacles are those frightful things you see when you take your eyes off your goal.

～ HENRY FORD

If you don't design your own life plan, chances are you'll fall into someone else's plan.

～ JIM ROHN

Don't let anybody take your dreams away from you. Talk about your goals. Let your friends and family know, even if they say, "Oh it's impossible." Nothing is impossible. Keep dreaming.

～ CELINE DION

four

PERSEVERANCE

Great things are not done by impulse,
but by a series of small things brought together.

VINCENT VAN GOGH

Don't Quit

When things go wrong as they sometimes will,
When the road you're trudging seems all uphill,
When the funds are low, and the debts are high,
And you want to smile, but you have to sigh,
When care is pressing you down a bit—
Rest if you must, but don't you quit.

Success is failure turned inside out,
The silver tint of the clouds of doubt,
And you never can tell how close you are,
It may be near when it seems afar,
So, stick to the fight when you're hardest hit—
It's when things go wrong that you mustn't quit.

∽ AUTHOR UNKNOWN

Thoughts on Perseverance

Perseverance is a great element of success. If you only knock long enough and loud enough at the gate, you are sure to wake up somebody.

∾ HENRY WADSWORTH LONGFELLOW

If you care about what you do and work hard at it, there isn't anything you can't do if you want to.

∾ JIM HENSON

Genius is 1 percent inspiration and 99 percent perspiration.

∾ THOMAS A. EDISON

Small disciplines repeated with consistency every day lead to great achievements gained slowly over time.

∾ JOHN C. MAXWELL

Abraham Lincoln

You can have anything you want if you want it badly enough. You can be anything you want to be, do anything you set out to accomplish if you hold to that desire with singleness of purpose.

～ ABRAHAM LINCOLN

Abraham Lincoln's background:

Was defeated in a legislative race at 23.

Went bankrupt at age 25.

Overcame the death of his sweetheart at age 26.

Failed to gain his party's nomination for Congress at age 31.

Lost a senatorial race at age 45.

Lost a senatorial race at age 49.

Was elected president of the United States at age 51.

Courage

You block your dream when you allow your fear to grow bigger than your faith.

∽ MARY MANIN MORRISSEY

Everyone has talent. What is rare is the courage to follow talent to the dark place where it leads.

∽ ERICA JONG

Have the courage to say no. Have the courage to face the truth. Do the right thing because it is right. These are the magic keys to living your life with integrity.

∽ W. CLEMENT STONE

Success is not final, failure is not fatal: It is the courage to continue that counts.

∽ WINSTON CHURCHILL

The Gift of Optimism

A pessimist is one who makes difficulties of his opportunities. An optimist is one who makes opportunities of his difficulties.

∾ WINSTON CHURCHILL

Optimism is the faith that leads to achievement. Nothing can be done without hope and confidence.

∾ HELEN KELLER

I am not discouraged, because every wrong attempt discarded is another step forward.

∾ THOMAS A. EDISON

Extraordinary people visualize not what is possible or probable, but rather what is impossible. And by visualizing the impossible, they begin to see it as possible.

∾ CHÉRIE CARTER-SCOTT

Learn to Love the Wild Places

Learn to love
the wild places
in your soul,
to cherish the hawk
whose wide wings
are your own.
Learn to trust
that trembling heart
whose swirling depths
call you to give
what cannot be given.
Let that eager mind
that rides the updrafts
soar beyond the known.

∽ SUSAN LANDON

Keep Trying

If your opponent is bigger, faster, and stronger; train longer, harder, and smarter.

~ H. JACKSON BROWN, JR.

Lasso your dream; hogtie it. Hold on tight and ride that thing as far as it'll take you. It may buck you a time or two; just dust yourself off and get right back in that saddle.

~ SARAH C. BLAKELEY

You should never let your fears prevent you from doing what you know is right.

~ AUNG SAN SUU KYI

The moment you commit and quit holding back, all sorts of unforeseen incidents, meetings, and material assistance will rise up to help you. The simple act of commitment is a powerful magnet for help.

∾ NAPOLEON HILL

Just don't give up trying to do what you really want to do. Where there is love and inspiration, I don't think you can go wrong.

∾ ELLA FITZGERALD

Success

Success means we go to sleep at night knowing that our talents and abilities were used in a way that served others. We're compensated by grateful looks in people's eyes, whatever material abundance supports us in performing joyfully and at high energy, and the magnificent feeling that we did our bit today to save the world.

◦◦ MARIANNE WILLIAMSON

five

EXCELLENCE

*The roots of true achievement lie in the will
to become the best that you can become.*

HAROLD TAYLOR

The Highest of Arts

It is something to be able to paint a particular picture,
or to carve a statue, and so make a few objects
beautiful; but it is far more glorious to carve and paint
the very atmosphere and medium through which
we look to affect the quality of the day. That is the
highest of arts.

∽ HENRY DAVID THOREAU

Wisdom

Don't go looking for a reward
just because you did "the right thing."
That *doing* is its own reward.
We shouldn't do good in the world
because we expect a return.
There's no deposit on those actions,
so don't go looking for one.
Do good and then forget about it.
Go on noticing all the ways you can help again.

∾ CORRINE DE WINTER

Build Something That Endures

Tentative efforts lead to tentative outcomes.
Therefore, give yourself fully to your endeavors.
Decide to construct your character through excellent
actions and determine to pay the price of a worthy
goal. The trials you encounter will introduce you to
your strengths. Remain steadfast . . . and one day you
will build something that endures, something worthy
of your potential.

∾ EPICTETUS

Thoughts on Excellence

Excellence is never an accident. It is always the result of high intention, sincere effort, and intelligent execution; it represents the wise choice of many alternatives—choice, not chance, determines your destiny.

∾ ARISTOTLE

Going far beyond that call of duty, doing more than others expect—this is what excellence is all about!

∾ JACK JOHNSON

The happiest and most contented people are those who each day perform to make the best of their abilities.

∾ ALFRED A. MONTAPERT

The hallmark of excellence, the test of greatness, is consistency.

∾ JIM TRESSEL

Be the Change

Be the change you wish to see in the world.

          ~ MAHATMA GANDHI

You're happiest while you're making the greatest contribution.

          ~ ROBERT F. KENNEDY

What is the use of living, if it be not to strive for noble causes and to make this muddled world a better place for those who will live in it after we are gone?

          ~ WINSTON CHURCHILL

Everybody can be great . . . because anybody can serve. You don't have to have a college degree to serve. You don't have to make your subject and verb agree to serve. You only need a heart full of grace. A soul generated by love.

          ~ MARTIN LUTHER KING, JR.

The best way to find yourself is to lose yourself in the service of others.

∾ MAHATMA GANDHI

I have one life and one chance to make it count for something. . . . My faith demands that I do whatever I can, wherever I am, whenever I can, for as long as I can with whatever I have to try to make a difference.

∾ JIMMY CARTER

We must not, in trying to think about how we can make a big difference, ignore the small daily differences we can make which, over time, add up to big differences that we often cannot foresee.

∾ MARIAN WRIGHT EDELMAN

Your Thoughts

The thought manifests as the word;
The word manifests as the deed;
The deed develops into habit;
And habit hardens into character.
So watch the thought and its ways with care,
And let it spring from love
Born out of concern for all beings.

∽ THE BUDDHA

Your Power

The greatest discovery of any generation is that human beings can alter their lives by altering their attitudes.

∾ ALBERT SCHWEITZER

When we align our thoughts, emotions, and actions with the highest part of ourselves, we are filled with enthusiasm, purpose, and meaning. . . . We are joyously and intimately engaged with our world. This is the experience of authentic power.

∾ GARY ZUKAV

We can't control our destiny,
but we can control who we become.

∾ ANNE FRANK

What do you want to do? What do you want to be? What do you want to have? Where do you want to go? Who do you want to go with? How the hell do you plan to get there? Write it down. Go do it. Enjoy it. Share it. It doesn't get much simpler or better than that.

∾ LEE IACOCCA

My Hope

Let me recognize, O God,
the good in everyone.
Keep me from a critical attitude
and inspire me to be open to all.
Encourage me to learn from others' ways
and to share knowledge willingly.
Bless me with a heart that loves,
hands that reach out,
eyes that see the beautiful,
and a voice that speaks of truth.

∾ THERESA MARY GRASS

Good Advice

I am always doing that which I cannot do, in order to learn how to do it.

       ❧ PABLO PICASSO

Follow effective action with quiet reflection. From the quiet reflection will come even more effective action.

       ❧ PETER F. DRUCKER

As I grow older I pay less attention to what people say. I just watch what they do.

       ❧ ANDREW CARNEGIE

When faced with uncertainty about taking a leap of faith, take the leap.

       ❧ CHRIS GUILLEBEAU

six

REFLECTIONS

Tell me, what is it that you plan to do with your one wild and precious life?

Mary Oliver, "The Summer Day"

A Piece of Parchment

They take up so few lines in an obituary:
"She learned five languages."
"He earned a bachelor's degree."
Head of the class. Certified.
A diploma. Degree by degree.

At the time, though, each tongue,
each certificate, each appositive
mattered, took time, made a difference,
and made a man or a woman
out of clay and a promise.

Hard, slogging hours of dazed days and
all-nighters ended at last in winning work.
Plus, yes, the mistakes and crashes
and humiliations, too horrid.

And, yet, and, more . . .
Here, says a sergeant-at-arms
or a principal in silken suit;
Here, says a college president
or the dean swimming in velveted sleeves.
Here.

It's nothing but a piece of paper,
maybe only a line in the end, but,
Here, this parchment is everything.

∽ Martha K. Baker

Florence Nightingale

Florence Nightingale (1820–1910) wrote the definitive *Notes on Nursing* and became known as the Lady with the Lamp while caring for the wounded at night during the Crimean War. She effected changes in the Crimea that caused death rates to plummet from 42 percent to 2.2 percent; her statistical charting convinced the government to reform care of wounded soldiers (she was the first woman inducted in her nation's association of statisticians). She devised a system of education that raised nursing to a profession, and she inspired a Swiss philanthropist to develop the idea of the Red Cross.

Nightingale became a blessed catalyst for change in the world (she actively nursed only two of her 90 years). She was a social activist concerned with the poor, especially women. She wrote 200 books; 14,000 of her letters are archived. She was also a theologian, a contemplative, "a God-intoxicated being."

She lived by this motto: "Be heroic in your *every day's* work, your *every day's* resolutions; even if you don't work up to them quite, you can do better each day."

May you live by her example. May her lantern glow in your service unto others and her life shine in your practice. May her compassion radiate in you who not only heal but also bless.

And may her lifelong illumination guide each nurse, every day, to do better.

∾ Martha K. Baker

Success

I don't know the key to success, but the key to failure is trying to please everybody.

~ BILL COSBY

One of the dangers of success is that it can make a person unteachable. Many people are tempted to use their success as permission to discontinue their growth. They become convinced that they know how to succeed and they begin to coast. They trade innovation and growth for a formula, which they follow time after time. "You can't argue with success," they say. But they're wrong. Why? Because the skills that got you *here* are probably not the skills that will get you *there*.

~ JOHN C. MAXWELL

Success is stumbling from failure to failure with no loss of enthusiasm.

~ WINSTON CHURCHILL

Failure is the condiment that gives success its flavor.

~ TRUMAN CAPOTE

A Lifelong Career

College isn't for everyone but education is a life-long career. Over the course of your lifetime, you have the freedom to study everything that interests you as much as your time and obligations will allow you. Magazines, books, online, the world is at your fingertips. Biography, history, science, adventure—it's easier than ever before to keep learning!

∾ SALLY CLARK

Divine Guidance

Be with me as I enter Your presence.
Give me the patience
and the stillness to hear Your voice.
Fill me with Your spirit,
and help me to understand
what You want me to know.
Quieten my noisy head to make room
for what You want me to hear.
Grant me the wisdom to do Your will—
this day and in the days to come.
Bring me a blessing today
and help me to recognize it when I see it.

∾ PHYLLIS K. COLLIER

Think About It

The Morning Question: What good shall I do today?
The Evening Question: What good have I done today?

～ BENJAMIN FRANKLIN

What matters most to you? How will you take over
the world? Most important, what will be the terms of
your unconventional, remarkable life?

～ CHRIS GUILLEBEAU

What would it be like if you lived each day, each
breath, as a work of art in progress? Imagine that you
are a Masterpiece unfolding, every second of every
day, a work of art taking form with every breath.

～ THOMAS CRUM

Instead of asking "What do I want from life?,"
a more powerful question is, "What does life want
from me?"

～ ECKHART TOLLE

Say Yes to What You Love

It is the greatest shot of adrenaline to be doing what you've wanted to do so badly. You almost feel like you could fly without the plane.

∾ CHARLES LINDBERGH

He was the first to fly the Atlantic solo nonstop. Charles Lindbergh dreamed of extending the boundaries of flight. When he landed his plane, the *Spirit of St. Louis,* outside of Paris on May 21, 1927, he became an international hero. He flew not for adulation or reward, but because he loved flying.

If there is a pure passion in your heart, it can often be a sign of what you are called to do in this life. Are you willing to step out in faith and say yes to what you love?

If you cherish a dream in your heart, trust that the doors of opportunity will open in unexpected ways in Divine and perfect timing. And then be brave enough to walk through those doors into a life of doing what you love and being who you truly are.

Is there something that makes you feel like you could "fly without the plane"?

∽ CANDY PAULL

Live Full

Live your beliefs and you can turn the world around.

∾ Henry David Thoreau

You will find as you look back upon your life that the moments when you have truly lived are the moments when you have done things in the spirit of love.

∾ Henry Drummond

Let us not get so busy or live so fast that we can't listen to the music of the meadow or the symphony that glorifies the forest. Some things in the world are far more important than wealth; one of them is the ability to enjoy simple things.

∾ Dale Carnegie

Making Life Worthwhile

May every soul that touches mine—
Be it the slightest contact—
Get therefrom some good;
Some little grace; one kindly thought;
One aspiration yet unfelt;
One bit of courage
For the darkening sky;
One gleam of faith
To brave the thickening ills of life;
One glimpse of brighter skies
Beyond the gathering mists—
To make this life worthwhile
And heaven a surer heritage.

∾ GEORGE ELIOT

Perspective

As a single footstep will not make a path on the earth, so a single thought will not make a pathway in the mind. To make a deep physical path, we walk again and again. To make a deep mental path, we must think over and over the kind of thoughts we wish to dominate our lives.

∾ HENRY DAVID THOREAU

Love and desire are the spirit's wings to great deeds.

∾ JOHANN WOLFGANG VON GOETHE

I long to accomplish a great and noble task, but it is my chief duty to accomplish small tasks as if they are great and noble.

∾ HELEN KELLER

What lies behind us and what lies before us are tiny matters compared to what lies within us.

∾ RALPH WALDO EMERSON

Expect Good

It is a funny thing about life; if you refuse to accept anything but the very best, you very often get it.

~ W. Somerset Maugham

Look at the sky. We are not alone. The whole universe is friendly to us and conspires only to give the best to those who dream and work.

~ A. P. J. Abdul Kalam

Expect the best; convert problems into opportunities; be dissatisfied with the status quo; focus on where you want to go, instead of where you're coming from; and most importantly, decide to be happy, knowing it's an attitude, a habit gained from daily practice, and not a result or payoff.

~ Denis Waitley

Everyone has inside of him a piece of good news. The good news is that you don't know how great you can be! How much you can love! What you can accomplish! And what your potential is!

~ Anne Frank

seven

INSPIRATION

Start small
Dream big
Live large

<small>JANA STANFIELD</small>

Stepping into the
Promised Unknown

May your lives open to all the sweetness
You have hidden away, fearing it might betray you

May you embrace each tomorrow
With wonder and delight

May your questions guide you toward humility
That you might learn to discern what is sacred

May you nurture the courage to choose wisely
So that justice and compassion might shape

The arc of your story, the circles
In which you are called to dance.

And may you learn to listen
To the whisperings of your angels

Urging you, as they do, to live ever closer
To the tremulous aching of your heart's insistent
    song.

∾ MICHAEL S. GLASER

As You Set Out

Let each place where you stand
    tell what it knows of you.
Let differences draw you.
Let the soil whisper
    to your feet as you pass.
Let the want of a place to rest:
    without bed
    without home
    without country,
elevate you to the level
    of kin to all.

Let the kindness of strangers
    feed your hunger
and shady grass beckon you
to lie down, be calmed
give over unrest.
Let each person you meet
ask something new of you.
With all that you see,
let wonder flow over you
    like mountain rain
    to wash you clean,
wash the dust of the road
    from your feet.

∾ MAUREEN TOLMAN FLANNERY

Seek Adventure

Imagination will often carry us to worlds
that never were.
But without it we go nowhere.

～ CARL SAGAN

Of course we all have our limits, but how can you
possibly find your boundaries unless you explore as far
and as wide as you possibly can? I would rather fail
in an attempt at something new and uncharted than
safely succeed in a repeat of something I have done.

～ A. E. HOTCHNER

The race will go to the curious, the slightly mad, and
those with an unsatiated passion for learning and
daredeviltry.

～ TOM PETERS

Face the world with arms wide open, and embrace it
for all it has to offer. Don't let go until you've tasted
every last drop.

～ SARAH C. BLAKELEY

Your Mission

When you know who you are;
when your mission is clear and you
burn with the inner fire of unbreakable will;
no cold can touch your heart;
no deluge can dampen your purpose.
You know that you are alive.

∿ CHIEF SEATTLE

Prelude

For the world will not applaud, though its
prizes, glittery honors, dazzling futures,
dangle like fat blue plums on faraway trees.
For every river you slog through, every rocky
hill you climb, what is attainable turns to dust
in your hands, ashes in your mouth, and
the world merely shrugs its beefy shoulders,
turns the spotlight on the next moth dancing
in the flame. Instead, think of spring, daffodils
and narcissus, tulips, azaleas, that flower
gorgeously for a few days, without any reason,
the April sky that draws over us its tender blue
blanket, the new grass green with infinite
hope. Consider then, trees that burst
into blossom: redbuds, dogwoods, magnolias,
such exuberant bloom, a carpet of petals
strewn on the sidewalks where you walked
to class. For the cold truth is, life on earth
is hard, love rocky and thorny and thistled,

but spring is renewable, an eternal library
book, from the first shy glimpse on the lawn,
to this grand finale of iris, peony, poppy,
this great commencement, this walk
in the sun. So may your roots find water,
good earth, work to do. May you blossom,
lavish and profuse. Never forget
that the heart is a flower. Go and dance
your hour on the lawn.

∾ BARBARA CROOKER

A Life Force

There is a vitality, a life force, a quickening that is translated through you into action, and because there is only one of you in all time, this expression is unique, and if you block it, it will never exist through any other medium; and be lost. The world will not have it. It is not your business to determine how good it is nor how it compares with other expression. It is your business to keep it yours clearly and directly, to keep the channel open. You do not even have to believe in yourself or your work. You have to keep open and aware directly to the urges that motivate you. Keep the channel open. No artist is pleased. There is no satisfaction whatever at any time. There is only a queer, divine dissatisfaction, a blessed unrest that keeps us marching and makes us more alive than the others.

∽ MARTHA GRAHAM

Be Bold

Most of the accomplishments I've achieved in life I began to attempt before I was really ready.

∾ JOHN C. MAXWELL

The greatest mistake you can make in life is to be continually fearing you will make one.

∾ ELBERT HUBBARD

List the things you would do if you weren't afraid. Then do at least one of them.

∾ JULIA SWEENEY

It is those with the boldest dreams
who awaken the best in all of us.

∾ JOHNNETTA B. COLE

Find Work You Love

The key is to trust your heart to move where your unique talents can flourish. This old world will really spin when work becomes a joyous expression of the soul.

～ AL SACHAROV

The truth is that all of us attain the greatest success and happiness possible in this life whenever we use our native capacities to their greatest extent.

～ DR. SMILEY BLANTON

If you have two or three real passions, don't feel like you have to pick and choose between them. Don't discard. Keep all your passions in your life.

～ AUSTIN KLEON

There is definitely a direct connection between finding your passion and reaching your potential.

∽ JOHN C. MAXWELL

Ask not what the world needs.
Ask what makes you come alive . . . then go do it.
Because what the world needs is people who have come alive.

∽ HOWARD THURMAN

I never did a day's work in my life. It was all fun!

∽ THOMAS A. EDISON

Do Something

One is not born into the world to do everything but to do something.

∾ HENRY DAVID THOREAU

This echoes a core belief I hope we share.

We're not here on this Earth to tackle *every* challenge. We're not meant to overcome *every* obstacle. We're here to do *one* thing. That ONE thing is something that *only we* can do.

I'm a firm believer that if more people had the courage to listen to their heart and follow their love; if they gave themselves permission to heal and forgive those who have hurt them in the past; and, if they had the courage to fulfill their purpose to help make the world a better place . . .

If you just took care to do that *one* thing, then our world would be a more peaceful, safe, and joyous place, for us *and* all beings.

∾ VAL HEART

Jump In!

The Law of Diminishing Intent says, "The longer you wait to do something you should do now, the greater the odds that you will never actually do it."

      ❧ JOHN C. MAXWELL

The thing that is really hard and really amazing is giving up on being perfect and beginning the work of becoming yourself.

      ❧ ANNA QUINDLEN

To dare is to lose one's footing momentarily. Not to dare, is to lose oneself.

      ❧ SØREN KIERKEGAARD

There is no such thing as a failed experiment, only experiments with unexpected outcomes.

      ❧ R. BUCKMINSTER FULLER

Never Dim Your Light

As you launch into the world
with your own personal trajectory
seek that which makes you comfortable
even if it's not what others would choose.
Admit your mistakes with grace,
find the power in humility
as you revel in your accomplishments.
Spill kindness onto the world,
don't let forgiveness be a stranger,
know that you are loved unconditionally,
and never, ever dim your light.

∽ MARILYN MACIEL

Be Extraordinary

You are capable of more than you know. Choose a goal that seems right for you and strive to be the best, however hard the path. Aim high. Behave honorably. Prepare to be alone at times, and to endure failure. Persist! The world needs all you can give.

∿ EDWARD O. WILSON

Life is a great big canvas, and you should throw all the paint on it you can.

∿ DANNY KAYE

Your playing small does not serve the world. There is nothing enlightened about shrinking so that other people won't feel insecure around you. We are all meant to shine, as children do.

∿ MARIANNE WILLIAMSON

There is no obstacle you cannot surmount, no challenge you cannot meet, no fear you cannot conquer, no matter how impossible it may sometimes seem.

∿ ERIN BROCKOVICH

Austin Kleon's Manifesto
from *Steal Like an Artist*

The manifesto is this:
Draw the art you want to see,
start the business you want to run,
play the music you want to hear,
write the books you want to read,
build the products you want to use—
do the work you want to see done.

∞ AUSTIN KLEON

Be Creative!

Many times we will get more ideas and better ideas in two hours of creative loafing than in eight hours at a desk.

◇ WILFERD PETERSON

The best way to have a good idea is to have a lot of ideas.

◇ LINUS PAULING

Creativity is the ability to pull things out of one's self or the universe or wherever you think this stuff comes from, and give it shape and form.

◇ WENDY HALE DAVIS

A hunch is creativity trying to tell you something.

◇ FRANK CAPRA

Become a Collector

Collect items you fancy and that for different reasons attract your attention. Remember also to collect and study things that seem for the moment to be meaningless and irrelevant. The twists and turns of the creative process lead you back to an important encounter that at first seemed quite neutral or even something that made you feel repelled or exasperated.

∾ Maja Ratkje

Tell Them Yes

All your life you are told the things you cannot do. All your life they will say you're not good enough or strong enough or talented enough; they will say you're the wrong height or the wrong weight or the wrong type to play this or be this or achieve this. **THEY WILL TELL YOU NO**, a thousand times no, until all the no's become meaningless. All your life they will tell you no, quite firmly and very quickly. **AND YOU WILL TELL THEM YES.**

                ~ NIKE AD

Connecting Dots (Or Not)

Creativity is connecting things. . . . You can't connect the dots looking forward. You can only connect them looking backward.

      ∾ STEVE JOBS

From now on, I'll connect the dots my own way.

      ∾ BILL WATTERSON

If you're worried about giving your secrets away, you can share your dots without connecting them.

      ∾ AUSTIN KLEON

Don't worry about people stealing your ideas. If your ideas are any good, you'll have to ram them down people's throats.

      ∾ HOWARD AIKEN

Five Life Lessons

1. *Laughter and Tears Go Hand in Hand*
Life is serious but it's also true that we can take ourselves too seriously. When we're tired, sick, or frazzled, we can focus on hassles and if we're not careful, act as though there were nothing else. Life has a way of wearing us down, if we let it. You may not be able to see the humor in your present situation, but never lose that ability.

2. *Be a Storyteller*
From beginning to end, our lives are stories, and so long as we can keep the stories flowing, we can stay lively and vibrant. Even if we find it difficult to tell happy stories, we need to keep the stories coming. When stories stop, something inside us stops flowing.

3. *The World Does Not Have to Stay as It Is*

Each of us every day has the opportunity to make a decision as to what energy, words, beliefs, and actions we will release into the world. The power lies within.

4. *Angels Abound*

I often think of angels as thoughts or impulses that tell me things are not as grim as I imagine. What makes the right person come into my life at the right moment and say just the right thing? Why, in my darkest hour, do the words "I am with you" explode in my head? I like to think that life is an ongoing communication with God.

5. *There Is a God Who Loves Us*

Some people have trouble believing in God. What we need, in order to find God, is a positive sense of mystery. In its positive meaning its synonym is "wonder." When we are overwhelmed by life, we have the ability to step back and wonder at the course of events. When we wonder about the course of events, we allow ourselves to slip into the realm of thought that holds perhaps what we see is not the whole picture. Perhaps there is something we do not know, a perspective not yet thought of, or a truth beyond our comprehension. I believe life teaches us lessons; the greatest lesson is that there is a Supreme Being who enfolds the mystery of our stories into the mystery of the Divine.

∾ PAUL KEENAN

Tikkun Olam

A Jewish belief tells us that we are all here to join God in repairing the world. Through finding our part in this quest, we complete our life's work and are renewed. Freedom comes when we let go of the ups and downs of our own personal journey and discover the joy and peace of being part of a larger purpose.

∼ DR. GREGG URY

Golden Rule

Kindness is at its best when we are dealing with someone with whom we disagree. Can we express our opinions to each other without putting the other down or insulting them? If so, that is the triumph of kindness.

∾ PAUL KEENAN

The real test of class is how you treat people who cannot possibly do you any good.

∾ AUTHOR UNKNOWN

In helping others, we shall help ourselves, for whatever good we give out completes the circle and comes back to us.

∾ FLORA EDWARDS

Ours is not the task of fixing the entire world at once, but of stretching out to mend the part of the world that is within our reach.

∾ DR. CLARISSA PINKOLA ESTÉS

Use God's Gifts

If you're blessed with a loving heart,
if you're caring, good, and kind,
with many strengths and talents,
and a smart, clear-thinking mind,
consider these as gifts from God
for you to use each day;
rely on them as you begin
the chase of fortune's way.
Do not forget to use God's gifts
in what you choose to be,
mix success with peace and love
and generosity.

Acknowledge that strong voice within
that tells you right from wrong;
console, encourage, lift others up,
and keep a faith that's strong.
Use wisely all God's gifts to you;
stay true to what you are,
and you will prosper in this life
as God's own shining star.

∿ HILDA LACHNEY SANDERSON

Proverb

Keep your eyes on knowledge;
Do not stumble, trip or fall.
Walk each path uprightly
And the world will see you tall.
Seek all grace and wisdom;
Hold to what is right—
Embrace the things you honor
And each day will be bright.
Love with understanding;
Smile with heart and eyes;
Your wealth will be well-being
And your vision reach the skies.

∽ JOAN STEPHEN

Success

To laugh often and much; to win the respect of intelligent people and the affection of children; to earn the appreciation of honest critics and endure the betrayal of false friends; to appreciate beauty; to find the best in others; to leave the world a bit better, whether by a healthy child, a garden patch, or a redeemed social condition; to know even one life has breathed easier because you have lived. This is to have succeeded.

∽ RALPH WALDO EMERSON

Do All the Good You Can

Do all the good you can,
By all the means you can,
In all the ways you can,
In all the places you can,
At all the times you can,
To all the people you can,
As long as you ever can.

~ JOHN WESLEY

You Can!

If you think you can, you can. And if you think you can't, you're right.

      ❧ MARY KAY ASH

Great things happen whenever we stop seeing ourselves as God's gift to others, and begin seeing others as God's gift to us.

      ❧ JAMES S. VUOCOLO

God's gift to us: potential. Our gift to God: developing it.

      ❧ AUTHOR UNKNOWN

Sometimes it falls upon a generation to be great. You can be that great generation.

      ❧ NELSON MANDELA

My Symphony

To live content with small means; to seek elegance rather than luxury, and refinement rather than fashion; to be worthy, not respectable; and wealthy, not rich; to study hard, think quietly, talk gently, act frankly; to listen to stars and birds, to babes and sages, with open heart; to bear all cheerfully, do all bravely, await occasion, hurry never; in a word, to let the spiritual, unbidden and unconscious grow up through the common. This is to be my symphony.

∾ WILLIAM HENRY CHANNING

eight

DAILY REMINDERS

*I consider the success of my day
based on the seeds I sow,
not the harvest I reap.*

ROBERT LOUIS STEVENSON

Act Enthusiastic and You'll Be Enthusiastic

While attending Bethel College in McKenzie, TN, a speech class was required as a part of my minor. The subject might not have been my preference, but the teacher certainly was one of my favorites. She was a delightful little lady named Ruby Krider. Mrs. Ruby could have retired years before but was still there simply for the love of teaching. When we would get up to give our speeches, one of her most memorable bits of advice was, "Act enthusiastic and you'll be enthusiastic."

At first, I thought this sounded a bit like "fake it till you make it." But the more that I thought about it the more I realized that what Mrs. Ruby was really saying was that you can't expect anyone else to have confidence in you if you don't have confidence in yourself.

You have to believe in yourself and in what you are doing before anyone else will believe it. As you present your product, your service, your cause, or even yourself to the world, be enthusiastic about what you have to offer. Self-confidence takes practice so if you act enthusiastic, the more enthusiastic you will become.

∾ SUE DAVIS POTTS

What We Do

Every day,
whatever we do
leaves its mark
on me, on you.

∾ CINDY BREEDLOVE

Look to This Day

Look to this day
for it is life
the very life of life.
In its brief course lie all
the realities and truths of existence,
the joy of growth,
the splendor of action,
the glory of power.
For yesterday is but a memory,
and tomorrow is only a vision.
But today well lived
makes every yesterday a memory
of happiness,
and every tomorrow a vision of hope.
Look well, therefore, to this day!

∼ ANCIENT SANSKRIT POEM

A Simple Prayer

Each day unique
Each day a choice
Each day gently
Each day loving
Each day ours

∽ ARLENE GAY LEVINE

In All Endeavors

In all endeavors
Strive to celebrate
The spirit of the warrior . . .
Calm,
Centered,
Certain . . .
Whether tending to the flower garden
Or searching for the heart of the divine.

∼ JO-ANNE ROWLEY

Think Big

Think big. Big things happen to big-thinking people. Nothing big happens to little-thinking people. You can become the person you want to be. It's possible. You'll discover this as you begin to break free from the tiger cage of impossibility thinking. Join in a grand adventure of discovering the beautiful life God has been planning for you. Join the exciting crowd of energetic, enthusiastic, youthful possibility thinkers.

∾ ROBERT H. SCHULLER

Fall in Love with
What You Do

How to never work
another day in your life:
Fall in love with what you do;
believe in what you're doing;
strive to continuously improve.

∽ BOB MOAWAD

Life

Life can be much broader once you discover one simple fact: Everything around you that you call life was made up by people who were no smarter than you. And you can change it, you can influence it, and you can build your own things that other people can use. Once you learn that, you'll never be the same again.

∽ STEVE JOBS

Daily Reminders

Almost every advance in art, cooking, medicine, agriculture, engineering, marketing, politics, education, and design has occurred when someone challenged the rules and tried another approach.

∾ ROGER VON OECH

Any day in which you learn something or help someone is a success.

∾ MARYANNE HANNAN

Follow your bliss and don't be afraid, and doors will open where you didn't know they were going to be.

∾ JOSEPH CAMPBELL

My philosophy is that not only are you responsible for your life, but doing the best at this moment puts you in the best place for the next moment.

∾ OPRAH WINFREY

When there's nothing you can do about anything, do everything you can.

∽ JAMES BROUGHTON

Let others lead small lives, but not you. Let others argue over small things, but not you. Let others cry over small hurts, but not you. Let others leave their future in someone else's hands, but not you.

∽ JIM ROHN

It's not where you take things from—it's where you take things to.

∽ JEAN-LUC GODARD

Mix a little foolishness with your serious plans. It is lovely to be silly at the right moment.

∽ HORACE

Our life is what our thoughts make it.

        ∾ MARCUS AURELIUS

No amount of success is worth your honesty.

        ∾ CANDY SCHOCK

I think of life itself now as a wonderful play that I've written for myself, and so my purpose is to have the utmost fun playing my part.

        ∾ SHIRLEY MACLAINE

Trust yourself.
You know more than you think you do.

        ∾ BENJAMIN SPOCK

There are only two ways to live your life.
One is as though nothing is a miracle. The other is as though everything is a miracle.

        ∾ ALBERT EINSTEIN

To be who you are and become what you are capable of is the only goal worth living.

◈ ALVIN AILEY

All life is an experiment. The more experiments you make the better.

◈ RALPH WALDO EMERSON

It is good to have things that money can buy, but it is also good to check up once in a while and be sure we have the things money can't buy.

◈ GEORGE HORACE LORIMER

nine

SUCCESS
BOOSTERS

To leave the world richer—
that is the ultimate success.

ELEANOR ROOSEVELT

Success doesn't come to you.
You go to it.

∾ MARVA COLLINS

Success is important only to the extent that it puts one
in a position to do more things one likes to do.

∾ SARAH CALDWELL

Life's only limitations are those you set upon yourself,
for as long as you strive hard enough anything is
achievable.

∾ CHAD WILLIAMS

Today is yesterday's results.
What you do now will be tomorrow's results.

∾ AUTHOR UNKNOWN

If you want to increase your success rate, double your failure rate.

                    ~ THOMAS J. WATSON

You *can* create the life you want, you *can* make the world a better place at the same time, and you *can* have it all. Just be prepared to work for it.

                    ~ CHRIS GUILLEBEAU

Don't just fly, soar.

           ~ *DUMBO*

The journey of a thousand miles begins with a single step.

                ~ LAO-TZU

Boldly walk into tomorrow with a purpose and a vision for a better world.

❧ HENRY LEO BOLDUC

There is no chance, no destiny, no fate, that can circumvent or hinder or control the firm resolve of a determined soul.

❧ ELLA WHEELER WILCOX

If you think small things don't matter, try spending the night in a room with a mosquito.

❧ THE DALAI LAMA

We make a living by what we get, but we make a life by what we give.

❧ WINSTON CHURCHILL

There is only one success—to be able to spend your life in your own way.

ᔰ CHRISTOPHER MORLEY

The secret of happiness is this: Let your interests be as wide as possible, and let your reactions to the things and persons that interest you be as far as possible friendly rather than hostile.

ᔰ BERTRAND RUSSELL

Every memorable act in the history of the world is a triumph of enthusiasm. Nothing great was ever achieved without it because it gives any challenge or any occupation, no matter how frightening or difficult, a new meaning. Without enthusiasm you are doomed to a life of mediocrity but with it you can accomplish miracles.

ᔰ OG MANDINO

Success is to be measured not so much by the position one has reached in life, as by the obstacles which he has overcome while trying to succeed.

∾ Booker T. Washington

We are what we repeatedly do. Excellence, then, is not an act but a habit.

∾ Aristotle

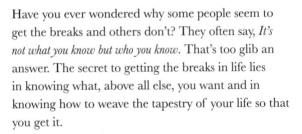

Have you ever wondered why some people seem to get the breaks and others don't? They often say, *It's not what you know but who you know.* That's too glib an answer. The secret to getting the breaks in life lies in knowing what, above all else, you want and in knowing how to weave the tapestry of your life so that you get it.

∾ Paul Keenan

Sparkle!

Share your sparkle wherever you are.

∾ DODINSKY

You are always on your way to a miracle.

∾ SARK

To infinity, and beyond!

∾ BUZZ LIGHTYEAR, *TOY STORY*

Author Index

Permissions and Acknowledgments

Grateful acknowledgment is made to the authors and publishers for the use of the following material. Every effort has been made to contact original sources. If notified, the publishers will be pleased to rectify an omission in future editions.

Martha K. Baker for "Florence Nightingale" and "A Piece of Parchment."
Virginia Barrett for "Feathers." www.VirginiaBarrett.com
Sarah C. Blakeley for "Face the World" and "Lasso Your Dream."
Cynthia Breedlove for "What We Do."
Sally Clark for "A Lifelong Career." www.SallyClark.info
Robert E. Collier for "Divine Guidance" by Phyllis K. Collier.
Barbara Crooker for "Prelude." www.BarbaraCrooker.com
Mary Maude Daniels for "Begin Again."
Corrine De Winter for "Believe in Something" and "Wisdom." www.CorrineDeWinter.com
Maureen Tolman Flannery for "As You Set Out" and "Find Yourself."
Anne Calodich Fone for "Waiting for You."
Charles Ghigna for "Ars Longa, Vita Brevis." www.FatherGoose.com

Michael S. Glaser for "Stepping into the Promised
  Unknown." www.MichaelSGlaser.com
Theresa Mary Grass for "My Hope."
Maryanne Hannan for "Any day in which you learn
  something" and "A Blessing for Your Dreams."
Emily Ruth Hazel for "Commencement" and "Wings."
  www.facebook.com/emilyruthhazel
Val Heart for "Do Something." www.ValHeart.com
Jacqueline Jules for "Tag Your Dreams."
  www.JacquelineJules.com
Susan Koefod for "New Experiences Ahead."
  www.SusanKoefod.com
Susan Landon for "Learn to Love the Wild Places."
Arlene Gay Levine for "The Call" and
  "A Simple Prayer." www.ArleneGayLevine.com
Barb Mayer for "Passages" and "Transformation."
  www.BarbMayer.com
Joan Noëldechen for "Destination."
  www.myspace.com/writingspaces
Susan Rogers Norton for "Destiny."
Paul A. Keenan Memorial Foundation for "Five Life
  Lessons," "Have you ever wondered," and "Kindness"
  by Paul Keenan. "Kindness" was excerpted from Paul
  Keenan's blog post, "The Triumph of Kindness"
  on June 3, 2008, one week before his death.
  www.FatherPaul.com

Candy Paull for "Say Yes to What You Love."
  www.CandyPaull.com
Sue Davis Potts for "Act Enthusiastic and
  You'll Be Enthusiastic."
Jo-Anne Rowley for "In All Endeavors."
Hilda Lachney Sanderson for "Use God's Gifts."
Candy Schock for "No amount of success."
Sherri Waas Shunfenthal for "New Directions."
Joel A. Singer for "When there's nothing you can do"
  by James Broughton. Copyright © 1997 by James
  Broughton. Published in *Packing Up for Paradise: Selected
  Poems 1946-1996* (Black Sparrow Books. Used with
  permission from Joel A. Singer. www.JoelASinger.com
Joan Stephen for "Philosophy" and "Proverb."
Paula Timpson for "Sanctuary."
  www.PaulasPoetryWorld.blogspot.com
Dr. Gregg Ury for "Tikkun Olam."

About the Author

June Cotner is the author or editor of twenty-nine books, including the best-selling *Graces, Bedside Prayers,* and *Dog Blessings.* Altogether her books have sold nearly one million copies.

June's latest love and avocation is giving presentations on adopting prisoner-trained shelter dogs. In 2011, she adopted Indy, a chocolate lab/Doberman mix (a LabraDobie!), from the Freedom Tails program at Stafford Creek Corrections Center in Aberdeen, Washington. June works with Indy daily to build on the wonderful obedience skills he mastered in the program. She and Indy have appeared on the television shows *AM Northwest* in Portland, Oregon, and *New Day Northwest* in Seattle.

A graduate of the University of California at Berkeley, June is the mother of two grown children and lives in Poulsbo, Washington, with her husband. Her hobbies include yoga, hiking, and playing with her two grandchildren.

For more information, please visit June's Web site at www.JuneCotner.com.

About the Author

June Cotner is the author or editor of twenty-nine books, including the best-selling *Graces*, *Bedside Prayers*, and *Dog Blessings*. Altogether her books have sold nearly one million copies.

June's latest love and avocation is giving presentations on adopting prisoner-trained shelter dogs. In 2011, she adopted Indy, a chocolate lab/Doberman mix (a LabraDobie!), from the Freedom Tails program at Stafford Creek Corrections Center in Aberdeen, Washington. June works with Indy daily to build on the wonderful obedience skills he mastered in the program. She and Indy have appeared on the television shows *AM Northwest* in Portland, Oregon, and *New Day Northwest* in Seattle.

A graduate of the University of California at Berkeley, June is the mother of two grown children and lives in Poulsbo, Washington, with her husband. Her hobbies include yoga, hiking, and playing with her two grandchildren.

For more information, please visit June's Web site at www.JuneCotner.com.